A RARE
MIRROR OF GOD

it's a collection of poetry, aphorisms and conversation between Man and God.

AFZAL ASKARI

AURAQ

Printed in the Islamic Republic of Pakistan.
Printed: March, 2020
Edition: 1st
ISBN: 978-969-7868-89 -6
Price: Rs 600 PKR, $6 US

AURAQ PUBLICATIONS

ISLAMABAD, PAKISTAN

raabta@auraqpublications.com.pk | +92-300-0571-530
www.auraqpublications.com.pk | @AuraqPublications
ISBN : 978-969-7868-89-6

TO MY LIFE, MY MOTHER...

TO MY HERO, MY FATHER...

TO MY HAPPINESS, MY SISTERS...

TO MY MENTORS,

ھے غالبؔ غالب ایسا کہ اب تک اقبال ھے...

ھے اقبالؔ کا اقبال اتنا کہ اب تک غالب ھے...

ھیں اگر شمس و رومی تمھارے لئے الگ الگ

تو کیا خاک سمجھے ھو تم ان کا فلسفہ

"You bear countless stories in yourself".

Said the Mountain and the Man on their first encounter.

On every page of this book there is a different story... Some narrated by the Mountain and some by the Man.

You exist in God's thought,
Enough for me to admire you....

All the dialogues of reunion,
Were never vital to desire you...

[7]

بستا تُو خدا کے خیال میں ہے

بس یہی یقین ہی تو میرا عشق ہے

تُو مجھے ملے یا نہ ملے

بھلا یہ بحث بھی کوئی عشق ہے

Forgive me Lord, for visiting my beloved
before you on Resurrection.
Given the ritual, you were discovered in the
same fashion.

معذرت خدا، جو ملا میں ان سے تجھ سے پہلے بروز حشر
روایت ہی دہراؤں گا، تو ملا ہی تھا اس کے بعد مجھے

Do not fall for the fallacy of remoteness my
beloved,
God too necessitates, not visibility but
imagination.

Hush, as silence is the finest narrator of all,
God too necessitates, not voice but
communication.

تُو پاس نہیں تو کیا تُو مجھ سے دور ہے؟
تیرا تصور ہی سب کُچھ، دِکھتا تو خدا بھی نہیں
تُو نہ بھی دے اگر آواز تو کیا میں انجان ہوں؟
تیری خاموشی ہی سب کُچھ، آواز تو خدا کی بھی نہیں

My stubbornness defines me,
I praise pain to preach peace.
I chase God to seek you.

ہے انسان کی ضد کا یہ انوکھا عروج

دلایا ہر مقام درد نے، تلاش پھر بھی سکون کی ہے

بار ہا سامنا ہوا خدا کا، تلاش نہ جانے کس کی ہے

Do not take my quietude as my attitude,
Lord.
Known is the felon, why to bother you.

میری خاموشی کو میرا غرور نہ سمجھ اے خدا

خطا کسی اور کی ہے، گلہ تجھ سے کیا کروں

Devastation is not the city where love ends
its pilgrimage,
It is the place from where love departs
from.

ہے بربادیِ انجامِ عشق پھر بھی کو دپڑے ہم
کتنے معصوم ہم، جو آغاز کو انجام سمجھ بیٹھے

My blooming desire in its odyssey ended in
wistful drought.
You being my only narrative and I the word
you never thought.

ہے بس اتنا ہی سفر میری خواہش سے میری حسرت کا
میں تیرا ہو گیا، تُو میرا ہو نہ سکا

Occupied is God writing my fate.
Curious is I, seeking you in every page.

اُدھر مصروف تھا خدا ہماری تقدیر لکھنے میں

اِدھر ہر صفحے پر ہم تیرا نام ڈھونڈ رہے تھے

Eden contrasts you sweetheart,
It is for all as you are for none,
but me.

آ بتاؤں تجھے کیوں ہے تُو جنت سے بالا تر

وہ سب کی ہے اور تُو صرف میرا ہے

The cosmos in its essence, is just an illusion.
Only You are the real art of God.

یہ جہاں بھیک ہے تیری، نہ کہ تیری دلیل خدا

افسانے کی کیا ہی اوقات، حقیقت کے سامنے

How can I unveil Her arrogance,
When the fabric is made from God's
forgiveness.

[27]

بڑے خراب پھنسے ہیں ہم سمجھ نہیں آتی کیا کریں

جتنے جتنے وہ مغرور اُتنا اُتنا وہ غفور

I was stranger to God's forgiveness,
Your footprints solved that mystery.

عشق مجھ گناہگار سے خدا کو کیسے؟

پوچھتا نہیں میں یہ اب تمہارے جانے کے بعد

There you go Lord, to conclude my
reverence here I kneel.
To conclude yours now, lift me up to the
one, we both wanted to steal.

ہوئی عبادت تمام، لے جھک گئے ہم سجدے میں
باری تیرے کرم کی یا رب، جو اٹھوں اب تو سامنے کوئی اور ہو

God conceals behind the messenger to
recall,
Love cost you your identity.

پسِ رسول تیرا پردہ اب سمجھ آیا خدا
عاشق کی کیا ہی پہچان معشوق کے سامنے

Creation contends to be your lover, God.
Obliterate reward to witness chaos.

بڑے دعوے تیرے عشق کے خدا مسجدوں میں ہر جگہ
ذرا جنت کی شرط تو واٹھا، تماشا دیکھنے کے لئے

To seek God, you have to seek that how He seeks you.

ہے فعلِ عاشقی نہیں معشوق سے روٹھ جانا
ہمیں تو بس یہی بات سمجھ آتی ہے ہر اذان کے بعد

Yesterday God narrated the story of Adam
to remind me,
Love being blind, doesn't mean it cannot
see.

نکال کر آدم کو بہشت سے خدا نے بس یہ ہے بتایا

ہے عشق بے لگام بیشک، مگر کوئی سلیقہ ہوتا ہے

Your arrogance is driven by my love
sweetheart.
I have played this game with the Creator
all my life.

[41]

ہے یہ میری عاشقی جو تیرا نازو نخرہ ہے عروج پر

ہے معلوم ہمیں سب کچھ، یوں ہی ہم بھی نمازیں نہیں قضاء کیا کرتے

Creation is too busy defining Day of
Judgment.
I am just excited to meet God.

ہے لفظ قیامت کیوں تمہارے لئے ڈرو پریشانی کا
ہم تو بے تاب ہیں خدا کی مہمان نوازی دیکھنے کو

Belief was never the answer, its submission.
Satan is not blind to the line.

ہے ذرا سا فرق خدا کو ماننے اور پہچاننے میں

ہماری بات کا اگر یقین نہیں تو شیطان کا ہی سوچ لو

I am familiar with the idea of God...
It is your concept that I cannot grasp on.

[47]

جانتا ہوں کہ خدا ہے
مگر تم ہو اس کا یقین نہیں آتا

God doesn't paint on my canvas anymore.
The colors you stole were his favorites.

خاموش ہو گیا ہوں تمہارے جانے کے بعد

کہا مجھ سے یہ خود خدا نے ہے

Dither not, to seek me in plight my beloved.
I too am shameless for God, in this regard.

تیرا میرے پاس آنا صرف ضرورت کے لمحوں میں

یاد دلا دیتا ہے مجھے، میرا رشتہ میرے خدا سے

The history of Man's ignorance is older than
man himself.
What else can be the reason of you not
being God.

ہے سیکھا انسان نے آج تک صرف لکیریں کھینچنا

بس یہی وجہ ہے جو تم اور خدا الگ ہو

I am stranger to Man's anxiety for life after
death.
Was he anxious too, before coming to this
life.

پریشان ہو کیوں بعدِ مرگ زندگی کا سوچ کر
کیا اِدھر بھی آئے تھے تم اس قدر سوچ سوچ کر

Stubbornness made Moses forget,
He had a mother.

حیران ہوا میں موسیٰ کی ضد سن کر
کیا نہیں دی تھی اسے خدا نے ماں

It is the same mirror.
Yesterday universe was reflecting
dichotomy,
Now unity.

صحیح و غلط ہے اب ورق پچھلا

تلاش اب لکیر کی ہے

Time is getting ready for its rebirth in the
cosmos.
Your love has cost me a new watch.

قصہ مختصر اس لمحے کا یہ
تھی ملاقات ان سے پہلی، خود سے آخری

Guilt shouldn't trick you sweetheart.
I have rejected myself too, long before you.

ایک تم ہی نہیں جس نے مجھے ٹھکرایا ہے

یہ حرکت میں بھی کر چکا ہوں

Love was excited to see its face,
Death whispered, we don't reflect.

گہرائی عشق کی رہ گئی معمہ

آدم سے اب تک جو ڈوبا، لاشہ نہیں ملا

We never talk to anyone but ourselves.

انسان کبھی بھی کسی دوسرے انسان سے بات نہیں کر رہا ہوتا، وہ صرف خود سے بات کر رہا ہوتا ہے۔

The Resurrection still awaits,
Is that not the Resurrection in itself?

ہے کیا یہ قیامت کم؟

کہ اب بھی قیامت آئے گی

If God too adored drawing lines,
Our cosmos wouldn't be painted in
gyrations.

جو ہوتی خدا کو بھی پسند اگر لکیریں

نہ ہوتی گردش میں ہر کہکشاں

Man in its idiocy shun himself,
in pursuit of purpose.

عمر گزر گئی انسان کی تلاشِ مقصد میں

جب کہ بننا صرف انسان ہی تھا

I have cried only one day,
The day I couldn't.

بخدا ہم بھی روئے ہیں بہت اس دن

چاہ کے بھی جب رونا نہ آیا

Only the graveyard of love is free from gravestones.

ہے یہ جرم ایسا جو ہستی مٹا دیتی ہے
صرف اس لئے قبرستانِ عشق میں تختیاں نہیں نظر آتیں

God is the echo of Love's whisper.

خدا گونج ہے، عشق کی سرگوشی کی

If you do not believe in God
You are upset from Him or yourself.

خدا کو نہ ماننے والا اکثر

خدا سے یا خود سے ناراض ہوتا ہے

You have to get crushed, to meet God.
Do not forget Mount Sinai.

[83]

یو نہی آتا نہیں خدا دل میں ہونا پڑے گا تجھے چکنا چور

ہماری بات کاا گر یقین نہیں تو طور کا،ہی سوچ لو

Seeking true God is insulting God.

ہے اگر تمہیں تلاش سچے خدا کی، تو تم خدا کو سمجھے ہی نہیں

The story of your betrayal is just a delusion, sweetheart
It was I, who lied to myself.

تذکرہ کیا ہی کروں خدا سے تمہاری بیو فائی کا

وہ تو میں تھا جو خود سے جھوٹ بولتا رہا

God: Reason of your cry?
Man: Fulfilled.

خدا : رو کیوں رہا ہے؟
انسان : بس اسی لیے رو رہا تھا

Human: I am alone...
God: Then whom have you whispered to?

انسان: تنہا ہوں

خدا: پھر بول کس سے رہا ہے؟

Human: You exist?
God: Existence is from me.

انسان: تو ہے؟

خدا: ہے مجھ سے ہے۔

Human: What is religion?
God: The longest path.
Human: What is love?
God: The shortest path.
Human: What is the path?
God: You

انسان: مذہب کیا ہے؟

خدا: طویل جواب

انسان: عشق کیا ہے؟

خدا: مختصر جواب

انسان: جواب کیا ہے؟

خدا: تو

God: Seek wisdom
Man: Why?
God: For the same reason

خدا: علم حاصل کر

انسان: کیوں؟

خدا: اسی لئے

God: What makes you arrogant?
Human: Imagining you.
Human: What makes you arrogant?
God: You.

خدا: تیرا غُرور کیا ہے؟
انسان: تیرا تصوّر
انسان: تیرا غُرور کیا ہے؟
خدا: تُو

Human: What would heal me?
God: Pain.

انسان: درد کیا ہے؟

خدا: دوا

Human: Am I?
God: Now you are.

انسان: میں ہوں؟

خدا: اب ہو گیا ہے

Human: I am in darkness.
God: Not now.
Human: I am sinful.
God: Not now.

انسان: تاریکی میں ہوں

خدا: اب نہیں

انسان: گناہگار ہوں

خدا: اب نہیں

To know or discuss the writer's
perspective about any part of this
book,
You can contact on

M.Afzal.Askari@gmail.com